Effective People Management

David Guest, Jonathan Michie, Maura Sheehan,
Neil Conway, Melvina Metochi

The Chartered Institute of Personnel and Development is the leading publisher of books and reports for personnel and training professionals, students, and all those concerned with the effective management and development of people at work. For full details of all our titles, please contact the Publishing Department:

Tel: 020 8263 3387
Fax: 020 8263 3850

E-mail: publish@cipd.co.uk

The catalogue of all CIPD titles can be viewed on the CIPD website:
www.cipd.co.uk/publications

Effective People Management

Initial findings of the Future of Work study

David Guest, Jonathan Michie, Maura Sheehan*,
Neil Conway, Melvina Metochi†

**School of Management and Organizational
Psychology, Birkbeck College**

* Department of Economics, Queen's University, Belfast

† Hong Kong Shanghai Banking Corporation

First published 2000

Designed and typeset by Beacon GDT
Cover design by Curve
Printed in Great Britain by Short Run Press

British Library Cataloguing in Publication Data
A catalogue record for this book is available from the British Library

ISBN 0 85292 887 4

Charted Institute of Personnel and Development,
CIPD House, Camp Road, London SW19 4UX

Tel: 020 8971 9000
Fax: 020 8263 3333
Website: www.cipd.co.uk

Incorporated by Royal Charter. Registered charity no. 1079797.

Contents

Acknowledgements

The research presented in this report is part of an ESRC-funded project on 'Workplace change, human resource management, and corporate performance', which forms part of the Future of Work Programme. The Chartered Institute of Personnel and Development provided further significant financial support to enable us to conduct telephone interviews and thereby to ensure a large sample. We acknowledge the support of both organisations.

Foreword

This report is part of a wider research programme being carried out by the Chartered Institute of Personnel and Development (CIPD). It aims to provide direction for managers seeking to optimise organisational performance through effective people management and development practice. Our hypothesis is that it is possible to build a framework of knowledge within which managers can make informed choices on what to do to bring about performance improvement based on the likely outcomes of appropriate and effective practice.

To enable us to do this we are concentrating our efforts in two main areas:

◻ the development of the body of knowledge

◻ identifying what the evidence means for practice.

There is already a large and growing body of evidence that demonstrates a wholly positive relationship between people management and development practice and organisational performance. This new work, the first large-scale, cross-sector survey carried out in the UK specifically to examine the impact of people management practice on business outcomes, offers an important new dimension to the evidence. It supports previous evidence on the people performance link; and it demonstrates that it is not just what you do, but how you do it that is important.

However, it is evident that the message is still not getting through to certain sections of the business community. Many proclaim people to be their greatest asset but they do not act as though they believe it. The evidence suggests that different

mindsets on this score would deliver a significant pay-off. People and development managers can and should articulate and drive the issues forward. The evidence helps them engage in decision-making as full business partners to ensure that the people dimension is considered on a par and within the same framework as other factors.

In addition, personnel specialists need to be more positive about developing measures to value the human contribution, as well as the processes they adopt to measure the effectiveness of that contribution. To help ensure this happens, our research programme includes extensive work on this theme, particularly why and how certain practices impact on business performance. We are also investigating chief executives' perceptions of people management practice and its role in organisational performance. This should help us to build greater understanding of why so many managers seem not to act on the evidence available and enable us to build arguments that will help to convince them.

This research shows that there is considerable scope to improve human resource management in British industry. Newly published research in the UK Aerospace industry[1] confirms the analysis. The challenge lies in making sure that any such improvement maximises the impact on business outcomes.

By demonstrating the mediating effect of a measure of effectiveness on the relationship between practice and performance, David Guest and his team not only improve the explanation of the relationship, but also help support the argument for integrated sets of practices. To achieve maximum effectiveness, practices must complement each other, be rooted in the same

1. THOMPSON M *The UK Aerospace People Management Audit 2000*. London, Society of British Aerospace Companies, 2000.

valued framework and relate in a managed way to business visions, goals and decision-making processes.

This piece of work is an important building block in a programme of work that will next include further analysis of the data in the light of more detailed financial information on company performance. This will add a further level of understanding about the nature of the relationship between people management practice and company performance, and will also provide guidance for our future work on process issues and on human capital. This exciting and progressive programme of evidence-led research is rapidly expanding and strengthening our knowledge and understanding of how to evaluate and measure the human contribution to business.

Angela Baron

Chartered Institute of Personnel and Development

Executive Summary

- This report presents the findings of telephone interviews with 610 managers responsible for human resource management (HRM) and 462 CEOs from a cross-section of companies in the UK. The interviews were conducted in July 1999. In 237 companies there were matched pairs of responses from both managers. The aim of the survey was to explore the relationship between HRM and business performance. With its overall coverage of 835 organisations, it is probably the largest company-level survey of this subject undertaken to date in the UK.

- The study was conducted within a model that examined links between business strategy, human resource (HR) practices, the effectiveness of these practices, the impact on employee attitudes and behaviour, and the consequences for productivity, quality and financial performance. Management descriptions and judgements about all of these issues were obtained.

- Business strategies in these companies give highest priority to responsiveness to customers, judged crucial by 74 per cent of CEOs, combined with a high quality of service, judged crucial by 59 per cent. In contrast, only 10 per cent considered that offering cheaper products than competitors was crucial to their success.

- Most managers only pay lip service to the idea that people are their most important assets. Seventy per cent say their organisations rely 'a lot' on people as a source of competitive advantage, but only 10 per cent strongly agree that people issues are a top priority ahead of financial or marketing issues.

- There is clearly considerable scope in British industry to improve HRM. The survey shows a generally low use of HR practices. Concentrating on a key list of 18 typical practices, only 1 per cent of companies have more than three-quarters of them in place and applying to most workers, and only 26 per cent apply more than half of them. At the other extreme, 20 per cent of organisations make extensive use of less than a quarter of these practices.

- Analysis of HR managers' responses shows a clear association between the number of HR practices adopted and the effectiveness of these practices. Both in turn are significantly associated with HR managers' perceptions of positive employee attitudes and behaviour, which in turn are linked to higher productivity, quality of goods and services and financial results. In other words, although at this stage we cannot demonstrate causality, the results show a link between HRM, employee attitudes and behaviour, and corporate performance.

- The most highly rated areas of activity are *labour market practices and employment security*, which is rated as highly effective by about a quarter of managers.

- Employee attitudes and behaviour are generally rated very positively. For example, about 70 per cent of managers rate the flexibility of employees to move between jobs as the work demands as fairly or very high. Seventy-five per cent rate the output and results achieved by employees as very or fairly high.

- Company performance is also assessed fairly positively, with 52 per cent of CEOs rating their productivity above average and 53 per cent rating financial results above average for their industry. In each case, only 8 per cent and 9 per cent respectively rate it below average.

- CEOs' responses show a similar set of links, except that they give more emphasis to the effectiveness (ie the quality) rather than the number (ie the quantity) of HR practices.

- On a number of issues, such as the existence of an HR strategy or the use of benchmarking, there is a rather modest level of agreement between CEOs and HR managers. This indicates a potentially low degree of consensus among the management team about some aspects of their work.

- These results, based on the descriptions and judgements of a large group of senior managers in British industry, support the view that the effective use of a wide range of progressive HR practices is linked to superior performance. This link includes taking seriously into account employee attitudes and behaviour.

- Since the general use of HR practices and their effectiveness in many organisations is low, this offers considerable scope to improve practices. On this evidence, British industry has not yet embraced HRM with any great enthusiasm. However, there is prima facie evidence that those who have done so achieve significant competitive advantage. This should therefore provide a wake-up call to the rest of industry.

- Further reports will analyse the association between the reports from CEOs and HR managers, and other, more-independent quantitative evidence of business performance.

1 | Introduction

◪ **A large number of studies provides evidence for a positive relationship between HRM and performance.**

◪ **Senior executives have yet to be convinced for reasons of scepticism, ignorance or prioritisation.**

◪ **There is no agreement on a definitive set of 'best' practices that will bring improved performance.**

It is a popular corporate cliché to assert that 'people are our most important assets'. A growing body of research evidence takes this a step further by showing that the way people are managed has a big impact on business performance. This report presents further evidence from the initial findings of a major new UK study exploring the relation between people management practices and performance. First, however, in this introductory section, we review the existing evidence and ask whether there *is* a link between human resource management (HRM) – the term now widely used to describe the management of people at work – and performance, and if so, how it might come about.

Good quality evidence about the relationship between HRM and performance is relatively recent. A series of studies in the United States, reported in the last five years, has found a link between HRM and performance, mainly focusing on measures of productivity (Ichniowski, Shaw and Prennushi, 1994) and financial performance (Delery and Doty, 1996; Huselid, 1995). At the same time, a smaller number of studies in the UK have also provided evidence for a relationship between HRM and performance (Patterson *et al*, 1997; Guest and Hoque, 1994, 1996). But while these results are promising, they have also

triggered an ongoing debate about key challenges to be considered when studying the relationship between HRM and performance, which the present study has sought to address. Many of these issues are raised in the recent review of the evidence prepared for the (then) IPD by Richardson and Thompson (1999) and are covered from a more academic stance by Guest (1997).

If the results of this initial set of studies are valid, and a distinctive approach to people management has a marked impact on corporate performance, then they deserve to be taken very seriously indeed. However, as the two reviews cited above point out, there are good reasons to be cautious; and as Pfeffer (1998) notes, top management has yet to be convinced. While it might seem no more than common sense to put in place a set of sound human resource (HR) practices, the evidence presented by Guest *et al* (2000) in their analysis of the 1998 Workplace Employee Relations Survey – with its coverage of 2,000 workplaces – shows that a majority of private-sector establishments have less than half of the core HR practices in place, and several have very few indeed.

Senior executives will have their own reasons for not always implementing the kind of HR practices that have been linked to high performance.

> "So what constitutes *good* people management? Clearly it is not just a matter of selection or job design, but going about these activities in a distinctive way."

These may be related to scepticism, ignorance, competing and more-important priorities, or the difficulty of bringing about the required change. For academics, the doubts are directed more at problems with the underlying theory, concerns about how to measure HR and performance and the way in which the research on which the claims are based has been conducted. Therefore, before describing the new study, which has sought to tackle many of these concerns, we briefly consider the nature of these challenges and how they might be addressed. We then present a model of the possible relationship between HRM and performance that provides an organising framework for our research findings.

What practices should be included in good people management?

Most organisations do some selection, training, communication and design of jobs. All have to decide how to reward employees. So what constitutes *good* people management? Clearly it is not just a matter of selection or job design, but going about these activities in a distinctive way. One argument is that they should all be based on some kind of underlying and guiding principles. One of the main choices that has been widely discussed is a distinction between an emphasis on *human* resource management and human *resource* management. Another way to describe the same distinction is to contrast 'soft' and 'hard' HRM. In the former case, the assumption is that HRM practices have an impact by seeking to achieve a fully committed, flexible and high-quality workforce, motivated and able to provide high performance. Practices are designed to achieve this; therefore, there will, among other things, be an emphasis on fair treatment, job security, design of jobs to promote autonomy and challenge, and scope for employee development. In contrast, the 'hard' approach is less concerned with creating a

climate of involvement and security, and more concerned with efficiently and effectively deploying people, as one amongst a range of business resources; it will typically emphasise the importance of performance management, the use of incentive payment systems and numerical flexibility. The work of Guest (1987, 1997), and the pioneering analysis of Walton (1985) is indicative of the 'soft' approach, while the work of American writers such as Huselid (1995) is more indicative of the 'hard' approach to HRM. While there are some overlaps between them, for example in the emphasis placed on training, they reflect rather different philosophies about the best way to manage people at work. Furthermore, they are only a starting point in guiding policy and practice and there are still areas of uncertainty about which practices to emphasise.

Are there distinctive 'best practices' or does it depend on the context?

Based either on some kind of underlying theory or on the evidence from research and practical experience, some writers, and most notably Pfeffer (1994, 1998), have argued that it might be possible to identify a set of 'best' HR practices that will result in improved performance. However, it seems that Pfeffer and others have a problem in agreeing on what to include in their list of 'best practices'. For example, should the emphasis be on flexible financial arrangements or on giving priority to internal promotions? The difficulty in identifying distinct 'best practices' is reflected in Pfeffer's own work. In his 1994 book, he outlined 16 practices, but by 1998 these had been reduced to seven, not least because several could be subsumed within a slightly broader classification.

On the other hand, as Becker and Gerhart (1996) argue, the idea of 'best practices' might be more appropriate for identifying the principles

> "**While research has presented evidence of the link between HRM and financial performance ... questions remain about** *how* **and** *why* **any association is found in the first place.**"

underlying the choice of practices, as opposed to the practices themselves. Accordingly, some writers (Becker *et al* 1997; Guest, 1997) have argued that HRM practices can improve company performance by:

◘ increasing employee skills and abilities

◘ promoting positive attitudes that result in a committed and motivated workforce

◘ providing expanded responsibilities that allow employees to make full use of their skills and abilities.

Is there added value from combining 'bundles' of best practices?

Another approach favoured by a number of writers is to apply systems, or 'bundles', of HRM practices, rather than focusing on individual practices (eg Huselid, 1995; MacDuffie, 1995), recognising that the whole is more than the sum of the parts. It is possible to have different 'bundles', raising questions about which are more effective. However, at the heart of any distinctive approach to HRM is a belief that a combination of practices is required. It is not enough just to do selection or training or appraisal outstandingly well. It is doing them all to this standard that will have an impact.

How does HRM relate to business strategy?

For some observers, the key issue for high corporate performance is the integration of HR strategy and practices with business strategy. By implication, since business strategy will vary, HR strategy and practice will also need to vary to fit the differing market conditions and the positioning of the firm in that market. In other words, the aim is to ensure 'external fit' to the market-driven

strategy. This has been central to much of the American research (Delery and Doty, 1996; Huselid, 1995; MacDuffie, 1995). Although there has been relatively little empirical evidence to support a relationship between this type of strategic integration and business performance, a belief in its importance persists among many researchers in this area. At the very least, it implies that we should incorporate measures of business strategy and HR strategy in our study.

A second approach places rather more emphasis on 'internal fit'. This is the argument that the various HR practices have to complement each other and that the philosophy behind them has to become embedded in the organisational culture to a point where it is fully accepted by line managers (Guest, 1987). Support for this position can be found in the work of writers such as Bartlett and Ghoshal (1989) and Collins and Porras (1994) who have examined successful companies, or what Collins and Porras refer to as 'visionary companies', and argued that the key to competitive advantage is to be found in the effective management of organisational culture and human resources. To reflect this, we need to build in a measure of HR integration, placing more emphasis on the way HR practices fit together than on their fit with business strategy.

How can we explain the link between HRM and performance?

A further challenge concerns the relationship between HRM and performance. While research has presented evidence of the link between HRM and financial performance (eg Huselid, 1995), questions remain about *how* and *why* any association is found in the first place.

This issue has been reviewed briefly by Becker and Gerhart (1996) and more extensively by Guest (1997), who has presented a model of the linkages. At its heart lies the view that HRM is essentially concerned with achieving results through full and effective utilisation of human resources. This is only likely to be achieved through a set of appropriate practices resulting in high quality, flexible and committed employees. They are likely to be more highly motivated and more innovative, resulting in a more productive but also more satisfied workforce. This is essentially in line with the 'soft' approach to HRM discussed earlier.

Recently, a growing consensus appears to be forming among writers that a variant of expectancy theory, as presented and discussed by Guest (1997) and Becker *et al* (1997), can provide one possible route to an explanation of how HRM practices have an impact on performance. Expectancy theory is concerned with the performance of individual workers and suggests that to ensure high performance, firms should ensure highly competent workers (through selection and training), jobs that give them sufficient autonomy and challenge to demonstrate their competence (through job design) and the kind of employment conditions that encourage motivation and commitment (through a positive psychological contract reflected in fair treatment, status equalisation and employment security). This is the 'soft' version of HRM outlined earlier and a key feature is that all three elements must be present together. By implication, together they are more than the sum of their parts.

What 'performance' should we be measuring?

If we want to explore the link between HRM and performance, we need to be clear what we mean by performance. As already noted, most research has concentrated on measures of productivity or financial results. Even in an area such as financial performance, there are issues about whether to measure return on assets or more esoteric measures, such as 'Tobin's q'. Researchers in the USA, in particular Huselid, are currently working on the refinement of such measures, but differing accounting practices in the UK and USA will make direct comparisons difficult. Furthermore, while we might prefer to obtain 'objective' data about performance, sceptics might argue that accounting protocols differ across countries so that firms can hide or move profits and losses. In other words, we should not always take the results at face value. Such information is also quite difficult to obtain. One alternative is to use subjective accounts of performance. When performance measures are collected at establishment level, this is almost essential. However, this introduces new issues of bias and subjectivity.

Leaving aside the difficult questions of the reliability and validity of data, there are further questions about which performance indicators matter. A stakeholder perspective would give some emphasis to performance outcomes of concern to the range of stakeholders. But use of a range of performance measures creates a risk that the indicators do not correlate highly – for example, productivity and customer satisfaction might not go hand in hand – resulting in a problem of deciding which indicators deserve most serious consideration. If we want to understand the reasons why HRM might be related to performance, we also need to collect performance measures for the range of possible linkages. Below we present a model that indicates that we need to measure: 'HRM outcomes' reflected in employee attitudes and behaviour; internal performance, such as productivity and quality of goods and services; and external indicators, such as sales and financial performance. In other words, if the research is to guide policy and practice, we need to collect a number of potentially related outcomes that extend beyond a narrow definition of business performance based just on financial indicators.

How the new study tries to answer these questions

The present study seeks to address many of these questions and challenges. It is based initially on the model presented by Guest (1997) of the linkages between strategy, HRM practices and performance. Aside from the question of whether HRM influences performance, we are also concerned with addressing the potential significance of strategic integration, both with respect to the coherence between practices and also with respect to integrating business strategy with HRM, and exploring the extent to which this translates in superior performance. Another factor that is incorporated in the model is the perceived effectiveness of the HR practices themselves and of the personnel department/professionals.

There are five main components in the model: strategy, HR practices, effectiveness of HR practices

and personnel departments, and HRM outcomes and performance outcomes. According to Guest (1997), performance outcomes can be understood in terms of internal outcomes – such as employee relations indicators, including labour turnover and absence, productivity, and quality of products and services – and external performance outcomes, including in particular financial performance. A range of background variables that may influence the relationship between HR practices and outcomes are also included, such as size, sector, ownership, business strategy, union representation and so on.

In essence then, it is proposed that HR practices will influence HRM outcomes, which in turn will lead to lower absence and labour turnover and increased productivity and quality; and these in turn should lead to an increase in sales and profitability.

Chapter 2 discusses in more detail the method employed to collect the data and describes the survey measures that were used to do so. It also outlines the structure of the rest of the report.

The study is conducted within the clear and testable framework in Figure 1. It will seek to

Figure 1 | Model of the link between HRM and performance

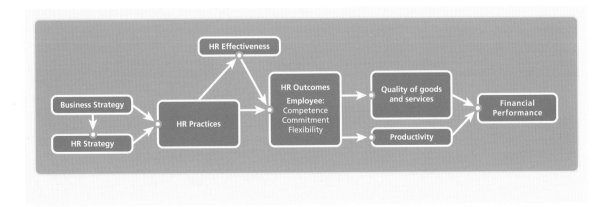

overcome some of the conceptual and measurement problems by using both 'soft' and 'hard' measures of HRM and both subjective and objective accounts of outcomes. As a cross-check, it will obtain information from both the senior HR manager and the CEO, or their nearest equivalents. It will collect cross-sectional information at one point in time and also collect data over time to gain some insights into cause and effect. Finally, it will complement surveys across industry with industry-specific detailed case studies.

This report presents the preliminary findings from the initial survey across industry, which has provided subjective accounts from HR managers and CEOs. There will be both a fuller analysis of these data and further reports once more objective performance data have also been collected. Indeed, the next report will link the subjective accounts of HRM and performance provided by managers and described in this report with the independent measures of productivity and financial outcomes.

2 | The Future of Work Study of Human Resource Management and Performance

◪ **Final sample comprised 1,072 respondents in 835 private-sector organisations with more than 50 employees.**

◪ **Interviews were conducted with 610 HR professionals and 462 CEOs.**

◪ **Interviews were carried out with 237 HR professionals and CEOs in the same company (ie matched pairs).**

◪ **Respondents were asked for their views on HR policies (both currently and in the future), HR strategy and business strategy.**

The research reported here forms part of a three-year research project, funded jointly by the ESRC's Future of Work Programme and the CIPD, and based at the School of Management and Organizational Psychology, Birkbeck College. The study aims to test the model presented in Chapter 1. The results reported here form the first stage of the analysis, and will be followed by a second report focusing on independent quantitative performance measures, such as published information on productivity and financial performance.

The first stage of the programme consists of a large national survey of private-sector companies designed to collect information on human resource (HR) practices and the strategic and organisational context in which they are applied. Information was also collected on assessments of the effectiveness of these practices and ratings of a range of outcomes, including employee commitment and behaviour, employee relations outcomes, and more conventional performance indicators. This information was collected from

both HR directors and CEOs, or their nearest equivalents. The rest of this report presents some of the key results from this survey, which is probably the largest of its kind undertaken at company level in the UK.

Sample and data collection

As already noted, the aims of this stage of the research were to collect fairly detailed information on HR practices, together with subjective judgements about effectiveness and performance from key managers. These will subsequently be matched to independent performance indicators. Although some queries might be raised concerning the use of subjective indicators, it is important to bear in mind that these may well be informed by more objective information and that key policy decisions will often be based on how senior managers view reality. Their beliefs and judgements are therefore of some importance.

One of the issues that had to be decided at an early stage was whether data would be collected at the establishment or company level. Given that one of our aims was to examine relationships between human resource management (HRM) and financial performance, it was more sensible to survey at the company level. This has potential shortcomings where we have to ask for general statements about HR practices across a number of establishments. But our sample is typical of UK industry and contains a large proportion of small and medium-sized firms, where this is unlikely to be a significant problem. Another influence on this decision was the existence of the Workplace Employee Relations Survey, which already provides somewhat parallel information at the establishment level.

Our initial aim was to obtain 350 matched pairs of responses from HR directors and CEOs. We used the Dunn and Bradstreet list of some 4,000 private-sector organisations and selected at random from this population, including only firms employing 50 or more employees. After a preliminary assessment of the likelihood of getting an acceptable response from postal questionnaires, which was deemed to be low, we used telephone interviews conducted by Taylor Nelson Sofres (Harris Research). The data were collected in July 1999.

Prior to contacting individual respondents, a letter was sent out to inform them that a researcher would contact them to seek their participation in the study. Each interview lasted between 20 and 25 minutes. To ensure the seniority of the HR professional, a question at the beginning of the interview asked whether the respondent was able to answer with respect to the *whole* UK-based organisation. If a negative response was obtained, the interviewer was instructed to request the details of the most suitable person and end the interview.

The target of 350 matched pairs proved difficult to achieve. Perhaps predictably, it was easier to contact HR managers than CEOs, resulting in some imbalance. Our final sample comprised 1,072 respondents in 835 private-sector organisations with more than 50 employees, across various industries. Our sample was equally representative of manufacturing and services, reflecting our interest in the private sector as a whole. In practice, given the contemporary structure of industry, this implies a bias towards the manufacturing sector. The 1,072 respondents comprised 610 heads of HRM and 462 CEOs. However, these were matched in only 237 organisations. As a result, in this report we will present some results for the large sample of HR managers and some for both the HR managers and CEOs in the matched sample.

In the matched sample, 80 per cent of organisations are UK-owned/controlled. They mainly range in size from 50 to 1,000 employees in the UK, with only about 6 per cent exceeding 1,000, and overall averaging 380. To identify any biases in the smaller, matched sample of 237 organisations, we carried out cross-checks, both with the larger sample of 610 HR professionals and the sample of 462 CEOs. These confirmed that the matched sample is 'typical' in terms of size of the organisations in the sample, the type of industry and ownership. More detailed background information about the different samples is presented in Chapter 3.

Questionnaire survey and measures

Initially, the Birkbeck team drafted two questionnaires, one for the CEO and the other for the HR manager. These questionnaires were then passed on to Harris Research, who in consultation with Birkbeck undertook a number of refinements.

The questionnaires were subsequently tested in a small number of randomly selected organisations to assess the suitability of the questions and to identify any problems with question wording. This led to some amendments to the questions asked and to the preparation of a glossary to accompany the questionnaire(s) during the interviews. The purpose of this was to eliminate any potential ambiguities in responding to the questions, and also to act as a guide in case the respondents requested clarification of the terms used in the questionnaire.

The involvement of both the HR manager and the CEO allowed us to explore aspects of the relationship between HRM and performance that would not have been possible with only one of the two respondents. It also allowed us to collect additional information that appeared more relevant for particular respondents. At the same time, several questions were identical, where we wanted to compare the responses.

The questionnaire for the HR managers asked:

- Background labour force questions: composition (part-time employment and short-term contracts), representation at the workplace (trade union recognition, single union/partnership deal(s) and the presence of a staff association), and redundancies.

- Questions on the use and coverage of HR practices in the areas of recruitment and selection, training and development, appraisal, financial flexibility, job design, concern with quality, communication and consultation, employment security, and single status and harmonisation.

- HR strategy and integration of HR practices with business strategy and with each other.

- HR outcomes, such as employee commitment, flexibility and behaviour, as well as the perceived effectiveness of the HR practices and the personnel department.

- Performance outcomes, such as labour turnover, absenteeism, and also ratings of the organisation's performance in terms of financial results, labour productivity, quality of products/ services and effectiveness of HR practices compared with other organisations in the same industry.

The questionnaire for the CEO covered HR strategy, a limited number of HR practices and the same items on effectiveness and performance. In addition, it asked for information on business strategy, on ownership and on the state of the market in which the organisation operated (competitiveness, market share, growth).

Both questionnaires also contained questions that asked their views on the importance of HR policies and practices for improvements in organisational performance, as well as the future use and development of these practices within their organisation and industry.

Finally, Patterson et al (1997) argue that one of the issues that researchers need to deal with is that of consistency of application of HR practices across different parts of the organisation, that is divisions, sites and product types. Acknowledging that this may be an important issue for our own results, we asked respondents to state at the beginning of the interview whether their HR practices 'differed considerably across divisions, business units and establishments in the UK'. The results show that at least for the purposes of the present sample, we can be fairly confident about any comparisons, since over 90 per cent of respondents stated that their HRM practices did not differ considerably across the different parts of the organisation.

The report framework

The report is organised around the model of the relationship between HRM and performance, presented in Chapter 1. This chapter is followed by a fairly extensive discussion of the descriptive results for each component of the model, that is strategy (business and HR integration), HRM practices and outcomes, effectiveness of HRM practices and department/professionals, and performance outcomes. This in turn is followed by a chapter containing the more complex analyses undertaken to explore the relationships posited in the model. It is important to bear in mind that although we may refer to 'causes' or 'antecedents', we are in fact reporting the results of a cross-sectional survey. While the conceptual model presented in the previous chapter implies causal links, we cannot confidently demonstrate a causal sequence in this type of study. The final chapter contains a discussion of the results and considers how much confidence we should have in them.

3 | The Organisations' Policies, Practices and Performance

◪ **In 52 per cent of organisations, the most senior person responsible for HR did not have an HR/personnel job title.**

◪ **Strategic priority is given to customer service, which is generally rated more important than cost.**

◪ **CEOs are more positive about HR strategy than HR professionals.**

◪ **The most positive ratings of effectiveness are given to practices relating to job security and labour market practices.**

◪ **Most respondents gave a positive evaluation of their employees and their company performance.**

In this chapter we present the results for each of the key components in the model presented in Chapter 1, that is strategy, human resource management (HRM) practices, effectiveness of HRM practices and the human resource (HR) professionals/department, HRM outcomes and performance outcomes. In the 237 organisations where responses have been obtained from both the HR manager and the CEO, we will present comparisons. We start by saying a little more about those who provided the information.

The respondents and their organisations

Of the responses obtained, 610 were from the most senior HR professional in the organisation. Forty per cent of respondents were either HR or personnel managers, and only 5 per cent were HR or personnel directors. A further 7 per cent had the title of personnel/HR officer. We do not know what proportion of those with a specialist title had relevant qualifications or CIPD membership. This leaves just under half the organisations where the person responsible for HR issues did not have an HR/personnel title. Instead, the most typical titles in this group were company director/secretary/

general manager, finance director, accountant/ payroll manager and other. One reason for this may be the significant proportion of smaller organisations in the sample. Fifty per cent of the organisations have a workforce of between 50 and 200 employees. The respondents were almost equally divided between men (49 per cent) and women (51 per cent). Although it is not always appropriate, we will use the term 'HR managers' to describe this group. However, when we undertake the more rigorous analysis, we will check whether the specialist role of the respondent makes a difference.

The sample of 462 CEOs is much more straightforward in the sense that 96 per cent have the title of managing director or CEO and the remainder were largely other directors. There is a marked gender imbalance, with 98 per cent being male. Eighty per cent work in UK-owned/ controlled organisations and for 81 per cent of them the UK accounts for more than half of their total sales. Finally, as discussed earlier, the matched sample is 'typical' in terms of size of the organisations, the type of industry and ownership.

Returning to the information from the 610 HR managers, as far as the composition of the workforce is concerned, part-time and contract-based employment is not particularly widespread. Fourteen per cent have no part-time workers, 62 per cent have between 1 per cent and 9 per cent, and 6 per cent have more than half. Fifty-four per cent have no employees on temporary or short-term contracts, 35 per cent have between 1 per cent and 9 per cent, and 10 per cent have between 10 per cent and 50 per cent. With regards to workplace representation, 66 per cent do not recognise a trade union, 20 per cent recognise one trade union, and the remaining 14 per cent recognise two or more. Even where trade unions are recognised, overall membership may not be high. In 42 per cent of such cases, overall membership is estimated to be below 50 per cent of employees. It is over 70 per cent in 29 per cent of such organisations, including 3 per cent where there is 100 per cent membership. Six per cent of organisations also report an independent staff

association. Sixty-one per cent of those recognising a trade union have a single-union deal. Thirteen organisations say they also have a partnership deal, though this question was only asked of those who recognise a trade union.

Strategy

Two aspects of strategy were included; one was business strategy and the other one was integration of HRM practices, both with each other (internal integration or 'fit') and with business strategy (external integration). This was an attempt to measure these two different aspects of integration, which were discussed in Chapter 1. In total, four items were used to measure these two aspects of integration and questions about these were asked of both CEOs and HR managers. Eight items were used to measure business strategy, but only CEOs were asked about this. The results for business strategy and HR integration are shown in Figures 2 and 3.

Figure 2 | Business strategy (all responses in %)

Note: CEOs from matched sample, N across items ranges between 190 and 237. Numbers are rounded and therefore do not always sum to 100 per cent (this applies to all subsequent similar figures).

Factor analysis shows that there are two main factors reflecting, as expected, a strategic focus on costs (alpha of .71) and on quality/innovation (alpha of .64). The final item cannot be sustained on its own and is removed from the subsequent analysis. What emerges from the responses in Figure 2 is the priority given to customer service. This is generally rated a more crucial aspect of strategy than cost considerations.

Managers were asked whether they had an HR strategy for their organisation. In the matched sample, 65 per cent of managing directors, but only 51 per cent of HR managers, said they did. This is an interesting difference of perception about what constitutes an HR strategy and implies that the results in the following section should be treated with some caution. One of the questions in

the section on HR strategy asked about Investors in People (IIP), since the existence of an HR strategy is a requirement to obtain IIP. In the full sample of HR managers, only 17 per cent claimed to have an IIP award. Intriguingly, 3 per cent said they did not know. Some of what are claimed to be HR strategies may therefore be only loosely delineated.

In Figure 3 we show results for perceptions of the integration of HR strategy for those organisations where a strategy was reported. Results were originally provided on a five-point scale. We have compressed this to three points for this presentation. Results for the managing directors are shown on the top row and for HR managers on the lower row.

Figure 3 | HR integration (all responses in %)

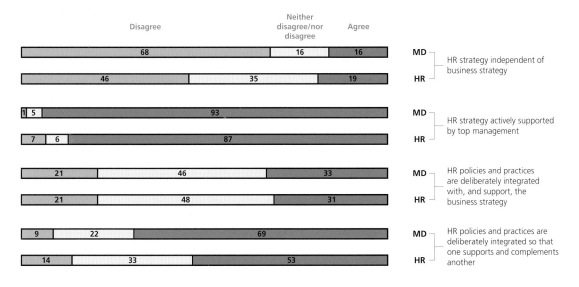

"CEOs are much more positive that
an HR strategy exists."

The results in Figure 3 reveal some differences in responses between the HR managers and CEOs. As we have already seen, CEOs are much more positive that an HR strategy exists. They are also more positive about its integration with business strategy and about the internal integration of HR policies and practices with each other. Despite the generally positive tone of the CEO responses, it is not wholly reassuring that only a third in both groups agree that HR policies and practices are deliberately integrated with and support the business strategy and that only just over half of the HR managers agree that HR policies and practices are deliberately integrated to support and complement each other. This implies that we may not find many 'bundles' of practices. It also indicates a fair degree of self-criticism, since there are few complaints about top management support for HR strategy. In the subsequent analyses we treat these four items measuring HR integration as a single scale.

While the responses of CEOs reflect a belief that HR concerns are well integrated into business activity, this does not in itself indicate that they regard HR issues as a key priority. This is reflected in the responses presented in Figure 4. The first question was only asked of the CEOs and it implies support for the importance of people as a source of competitive advantage. But when this is

pursued a little further in the second question, it appears that despite the popular rhetoric, in the majority of organisations people issues are not viewed by top managers as their most important assets.

HRM practices

A total of 48 items were used to measure HR practices. These were divided into the following sections:

◘ recruitment and selection

◘ training and development

◘ appraisal

◘ financial flexibility

◘ job design

◘ concern with quality

◘ communication and consultation

◘ employment security

◘ single status and harmonisation.

Figure 4 | People as a source of competitive advantage (all responses in %)

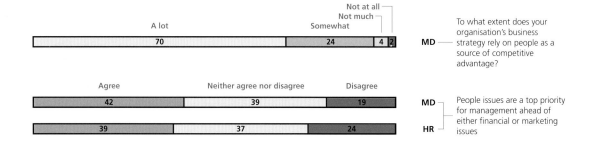

"Despite the popular rhetoric, in the majority of organisations people issues are not viewed by top managers as their most important assets."

We have already described some of the additional information we collected about trade unions and employment relations practices, and about employment flexibility. Some of the questions about practices were asked of both HR managers and CEOs. However, the majority were restricted to those responsible for HRM. Since we are interested in the influence of the full range of practices, we concentrate on the information provided by the HR managers. The pattern of responses in the full sample of HR managers and the matched sub-sample were almost identical, so we report the information from the full sample.

The responses sought varied depending on what was most appropriate. For some practices, we asked what proportion of the workforce they applied to. Figure 5 shows breakdowns of responses into those who used the practice for none of the workforce, a small proportion, a moderate proportion, and for almost everyone. For

a few items, frequency or duration was more appropriate than coverage of application. Finally, for a number of items it was only appropriate to provide a yes/no answer. For example, single status applies to everyone or else it cannot exist.

The full set of responses for the 48 items are shown in the Appendix. In addition to this full list, we constructed an index of key items. For each of the nine areas of HR practice listed above, we asked a number of questions. We decided to take the two from each section that were most representative. This was determined by statistical analysis to identify the two items that correlated most strongly with the overall score for that set of practices. A further check confirms that these 18 items correlate .90 with the overall set of 48 items, so we can be confident that they are representative. To avoid a completely unwieldy figure, it is these 18 key items that are presented in Figure 5.

Figure 5 | HR Practices (all responses in %)

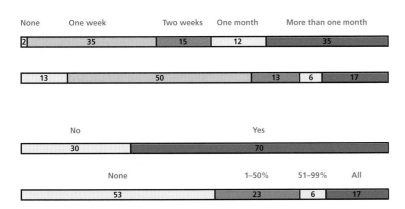

Training and Development

Training days given in the first year of employment to a new employee for the positions for which your organisation recruits in the largest numbers

Training days per year for experienced employees in those positions

Recruitment and Selection

There is a deliberate attempt to provide a preview of what work in the organisation will be like, including the more negative aspects, as part of the recruitment and selection process

Percentage of permanent recruits given a performance, ability or personality test as part of their selection

Figure 5 (continued) | HR Practices

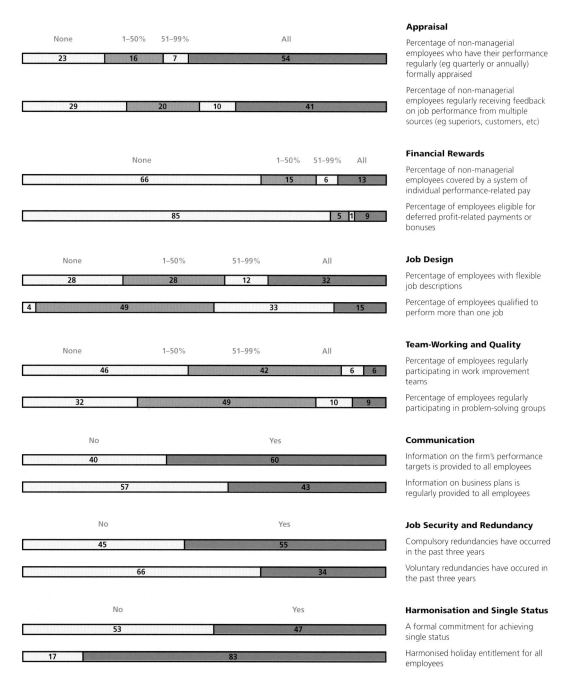

Note: N across items ranges between 576 and 610.

"**Only 1.1 per cent of organisations have more than
three-quarters of the key practices in place**"

Figure 6 | Number of HR practices in companies

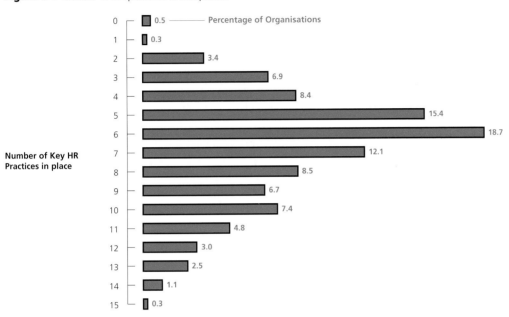

We undertook a factor analysis of the HR practices
to determine whether the items hung together to
form distinctive clusters or 'bundles'. This was not
very successful. Any factors that emerged did not fall
into a meaningful pattern. Therefore we have used a
count of practices. We had a choice about what sort
of 'cut-off' to use to determine whether a practice
was applied in a company. A cut-off at 10 per cent
would indicate whether a practice was used at all in
the organisation, but it might mean that it is just
applied to senior managers. A cut-off at around 50
per cent reveals widespread use, but the focus of
application is unclear. A cut-off at 90 per cent
indicates that the practice is prevalent throughout
the organisation. Since one of the core assumptions
of HRM is the application to the whole workforce of
practices that previously might only have been
applied to managers and professionals, this offers
the most interesting test. We therefore chose a 90
per cent cut-off as our criterion for whether the
practice was in place or not. Not surprisingly given
this strict test, the extent of application was quite

low. Using the 18 core items in Figure 5, we can
get an assessment of how far HRM is implemented
in these organisations. The results are shown in
Figure 6.

The index of 18 key practices is revealing. If we
take the full sample of 610 organisations, none
has more than 15 in place (we took no
redundancies as a positive practice). The median is
six practices. Put another way, 20 per cent of the
organisations have less than a quarter of the
practices in place, 74 per cent have less than half
and only 1.4 per cent, or nine organisations, have
more than three-quarters in place. We should not
necessarily expect to find all the practices in place.
For example, some are concerned with a 'hard'
version of HRM with its emphasis on performance
management, while others are more typical of a
'soft' model with a greater emphasis on the
elicitation of commitment. Leaving this aside, the
results still indicate a low application of HR
practices across this sample of UK organisations.

The effectiveness of HRM

Most previous studies of the relationship between HRM and performance have neglected the issue of HR effectiveness. While the assessment of the number of progressive practices or the identification of key bundles of practices can be linked directly to outcomes, it seems sensible to check whether the practices are judged to be implemented effectively. In this study, we asked both the HR managers and the CEOs to offer a view on the effectiveness of the practices and of the personnel department. The results are shown in Figures 7 and 8 (on pages 19 and 21). Once again we show them for the matched pairs that form the main focus of interest with the CEO/MD responses on top and the HR manager responses below.

In most cases, practices are judged to be 'slightly' or 'quite' effective. The most positive ratings of effectiveness, somewhat surprisingly, are given to *employment security and labour market practices*. The least effective ratings are given to *financial flexibility* and *job design*. Differences between CEOs and HR managers are generally small, though HR managers tend to be slightly more critical. These results fall well short of a ringing endorsement of the effectiveness of HRM.

All those interviewed were also asked to assess the effectiveness of 'the personnel/human resource department/professionals' across the areas in Figure 8. Once again the CEO/MD results are shown first and the HR manager responses below for the matched pairs. There are few differences between them in their assessments of this set of items. On most issues the department and its staff are judged to be only 'slightly' or 'quite' effective. Only on *maintaining up-to-date workforce*

"Most previous studies of the relationship between HRM and performance have neglected the issue of HR effectiveness."

Figure 7 | Effectiveness of HR practices (all responses in %)

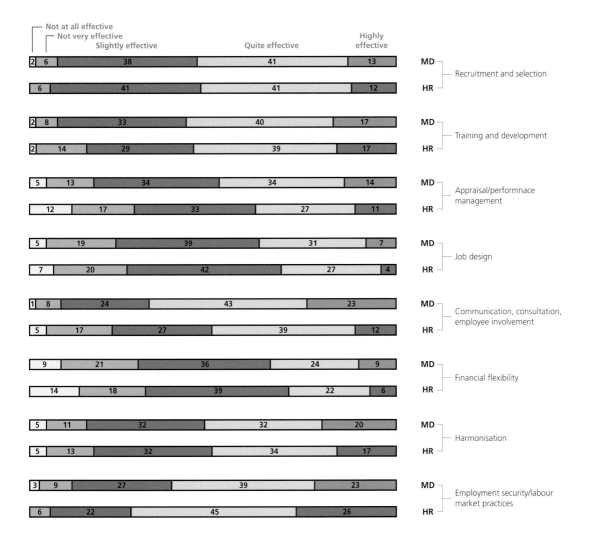

information, arguably not a core criterion for overall assessment, is there about a quarter of CEOs and HR managers saying 'highly' effective. The responses concerning effectiveness with progressing HR projects and initiatives are disappointing. Therefore, once again the responses, including those from managers responsible for HR departments, fall far short of enthusiastic support for the effectiveness of the department and the HR professionals in it.

We undertook a factor analysis of all the items concerned with effectiveness. This confirmed that all the items in Figure 7 formed one factor concerned with the effectiveness of HR practices (alpha of .81), so we combined these into a single measure of the effectiveness of HR practices for use in subsequent analysis. The factor analysis also confirmed that all the items in Figure 8 formed a second separate factor (alpha of .85) concerned with the effectiveness of HR processes carried out by the personnel/HR department and professionals. So we once again combined these into a single measure of the effectiveness of the personnel/HR department for all subsequent analyses.

HR outcomes

We collected information on a range of employee attitudes and behaviours. These included the commitment, quality and flexibility of employees and also their motivation, innovative behaviour and general performance. There are eight items in all, which are shown in Figure 9 (see page 23).

Figure 8 | Ratings of personnel department effectiveness (all responses in %)

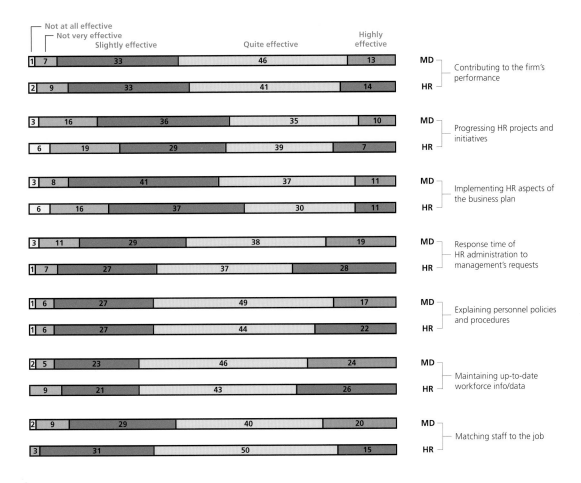

We again undertook a factor analysis of these responses, based on the full sample of HR managers, to see whether we could identify distinctive groupings. The outcome revealed two factors, one concerned with a combination of commitment, quality and contribution, which contains the first five items in Figure 9, and another containing the last three items and concerned with flexibility. (Alphas of .76 and .64 respectively based on the responses of all the HR managers and .77 and .74 based on the responses of all the CEOs.) We will use these two measures as indicators of HR outcomes in the subsequent analysis.

The assessment of employee-related outcomes, reflecting management judgements of employee attitudes and behaviour, are highly positive. The only areas where there is a sign of a negative response concern the levels of innovative behaviour and the ability to adjust the size of the workforce. Arguably, this last item is not really an indicator of employee behaviour. The other interesting finding is that the CEOs are more positive than the HR managers on most of the items.

Labour turnover, absence, grievances and industrial action

In addition to the assessments of employee attitudes and behaviour, we also collected information on a number of employee relations outcomes, including labour turnover, absence and grievances. This information was only collected from the HR managers.

Figure 9 | HR outcomes (all responses in %)

Commitment, Quality and Contribution

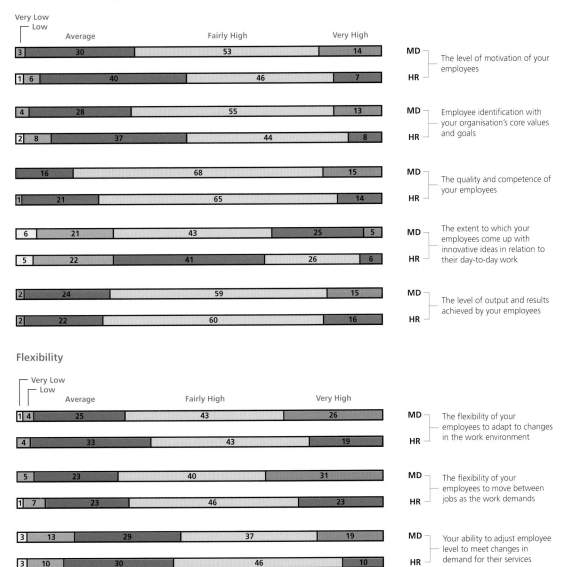

Flexibility

Labour turnover

The responses, for the full sample of 610 HR managers, show that labour turnover during the previous year, 1998, averaged 12.4 per cent. This hid a wide variation. Twenty-six per cent of organisations had a labour turnover of 4 per cent or less, while 10 per cent had a labour turnover above 30 per cent. Eleven per cent of HR managers did not know their firm's level of labour turnover in the previous year. It tended to be higher in services than in manufacturing firms. The more important question is how this related to the level they wanted. Thirty-five per cent said it was more than they wanted, 59 per cent said it was about right and 6 per cent said it was too low. Larger firms were more likely to indicate that labour turnover was higher than they wanted.

Absence levels

The average level of absence attributed to all causes was 8.1 per cent of working days. Again this reflected a wide range, from 28 per cent who lost 4 per cent of days or less to 6 per cent of firms who lost 20 per cent of days or more. However, this hides the fact that a further 41 per cent of those responsible for HR matters did not know their levels of absence in the previous year. This rose to over half of those working in the services sector. Absence levels tended to be slightly lower in larger organisations.

Grievances

Ninety-one per cent of organisations have a formal grievance system to which all employees have access. The average number of formal complaints in the previous year was 4.3, ranging from none to over 50. However, this needs to be linked to size of organisation to have much meaning.

Industrial conflict

Fifteen of the organisations, or 2 per cent, reported that there had been at least one serious incidence of industrial conflict in the previous year. This shows that organised conflict is now relatively rare and therefore decreasingly useful as an indicator of the state of employment relations.

These measures of employment relations outcomes are not central to the analysis, but we have the opportunity to examine any factors that explain variations in any of them.

Performance outcomes

The full study will include independent indicators of productivity and financial performance. In this first phase, we obtained ratings of comparative performance from managers. This approach is similar to that used in other survey studies, such as the Workplace Employee Relations Survey (Cully *et al* 1999). The questions asked for estimates about performance compared with other organisations in the same industry. We might expect some bias in the responses, but we expect it to be a consistent bias across organisations. Furthermore, a number of organisations undertake some form of benchmarking, which might enhance the accuracy of the information on which estimates are based. For example, 41 per cent of HR managers and 63 per cent of CEOs say their organisation benchmarks financial performance,

Figure 10 | Comparative performance (all responses in %)

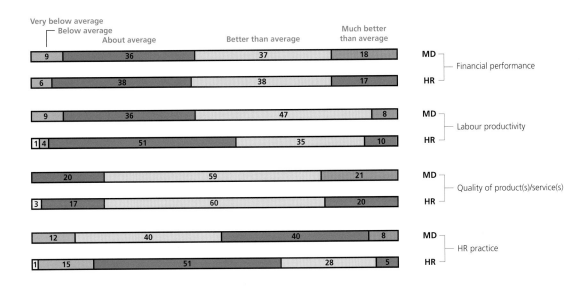

and 35 per cent of HR managers and 44 per cent of CEOs say they benchmark labour productivity. These variations in reports about the use of benchmarking are interesting in their own right and may reflect different views about what is meant by benchmarking

The results for comparative performance are shown in Figure 10. They confirm that many managers believe that their company performance is above average for their industry. Interestingly, they are least likely to be positive with respect to comparative performance on HR practices. This reinforces the doubts reported earlier about the effectiveness of HR practices and HR departments.

Summary

This chapter has summarised the findings for some of the core elements in the survey. It has concentrated on the main elements in the model linking HR practices and performance. It has confirmed only a moderate adoption of HR practices, a modest rating of their effectiveness and that of the HR department, but a generally positive evaluation of their employees and their company performance. Whether there is a link between practices, effectiveness, employee behaviour and business performance is the issue we explore in Chapter 4.

4 | The Link between Human Resource Management and Performance

- ◪ **There is strong endorsement of the model linking HRM and performance.**

- ◪ **The impact of HR practice on performance is indirect through its apparent impact on employee commitment, quality and flexibility.**

- ◪ **The measure of HR effectiveness improved our ability to explain the relationship between HRM and performance.**

- ◪ **Greater use of HR practice is associated with higher levels of effectiveness.**

- ◪ **The effectiveness of HR practices and HR functions is an important factor in explaining variations in company productivity and performance.**

Introduction

In this chapter we present a series of results examining the association between the adoption of more human resource (HR) practices and a range of outcomes. The outcomes are those identified in the model described in Chapter 2. In other words, we are interested in whether greater use of human resource management (HRM) and the effective application of HRM leads to reports of higher levels of commitment, contribution and flexible behaviour among employees and whether this in turn is associated with higher levels of productivity, quality of goods and services, and financial performance in a firm.

Because the sample and the data are complex, we present the results in a series of steps. First we explore the results for the full sample of 610 HR managers using a conventional analysis that focuses on the HR practices rather than on their effectiveness. We then add in the effectiveness of HR, since, as noted earlier, this is often neglected in the analysis of any association between HRM and performance. The next step is to analyse the data for the matched sample of 237 HR managers. This is a slightly more sophisticated analysis because we can incorporate background information derived from the CEO questionnaires about business strategy. Finally, we present the most rigorous test by taking HR managers' accounts of HR practices and incorporating them with the CEO reports on outcomes.

It is important at the outset to emphasise once again that we are dealing with cross-sectional results based on reports from managers. We therefore have to be very cautious about asserting cause and effect. On the basis of this analysis, we may find an association between greater use of HR practices and superior performance. But we cannot assert with confidence that the use of HR practices *caused* the increase in performance. Once it has been possible to collect performance data over a period of time, future reports will be able to examine the question of cause and effect with more confidence.

HRM and performance: the analysis for the 610 HR managers

For this sample of 610 HR managers, we collected only limited information on strategy, so the analysis concentrates on the core issue of the link between HRM and performance without incorporating measures of business and HR strategy or the strategic integration of HR. To assess this link, we undertook a standard linear regression. This controls for a number of

background factors, enabling us to test whether HR practices have an independent effect on employee attitudes and behaviour, productivity and so on. The results for the test of the full model are shown in Figure 11.

The results presented in Figure 11 provide a strong endorsement of the model presented in Chapter 2, which seeks to explain how HR practices and corporate performance might be linked. The model proposes that HR practices have an impact on employees' attitudes and behaviour, which in turn affect productivity and quality of goods and services, which then feeds through to financial performance. (Figure 11 shows the statistically significant associations, the numbers are beta weights and give a rough indication of the size of the association, while the asterisks indicate the level of statistical significance, with more asterisks indicating higher significance. Only significant links are shown.) Essentially, Figure 11 shows that

Figure 11 | HRM and performance (610 HR managers)

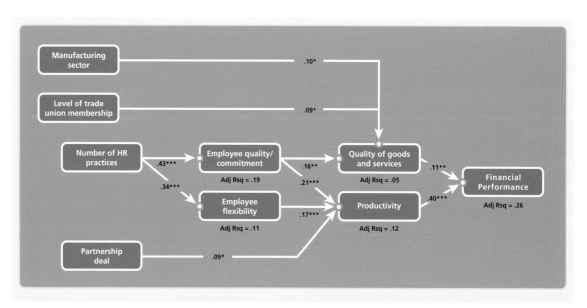

Note: * significant (p<0.05); ** strongly significant (p<0.01); *** very strongly significant (p<0.001).

greater use of HR practices is associated with higher levels of employee commitment and contribution and greater flexibility. Employee commitment and contribution is, in turn, associated with higher levels of reported productivity and quality of goods and services compared with major competitors; employee flexibility is also associated with higher productivity. Finally, productivity and quality of goods and services are associated with higher estimates of comparative financial performance.

There are a few additional factors that come into play. Partnership deals, which are very thin on the ground, are nevertheless associated with higher productivity. It is interesting that this is a direct link to productivity rather than a link through employee commitment. It could imply that the mutuality that is supposed (according to the popular Involvement and Participation Association (IPA) model) to inform partnership is perhaps a little one-sided. Employers gain productivity; employees gain no increase in commitment or quality. The other significant link reveals that quality of goods and services is considered to be higher in the manufacturing sector compared to the services sector and higher where there is a stronger trade union presence. The nature of the analysis indicates that the positive link to trade union density cannot simply be explained by the fact that trade unions are stronger in the manufacturing sector.

Although they are not reported in the model, we did analyse influences on the employment relations outcomes of labour turnover, absence and grievances. In doing so, we should bear in mind that many managers were unable to provide reliable information, more particularly about absence levels. It is perhaps not altogether surprising, therefore, that the background

variables explained no significant variation in reported levels of absence. However, they explained 10 per cent of the variation in labour turnover. The results indicate that labour turnover was lower in larger organisations (beta −16***), in manufacturing organisations (−11**), in organisations where there was a consultative system (−18***) and where there was a high level of employee commitment and contribution (−14*). Labour turnover was higher where there was a personnel professional in charge of the function (.10*).

The background variables explained 13 per cent of the variation in grievances. Grievance levels were lower in larger organisations (−27***), but higher where there was a consultative system (.10*) and where there was a professional in charge of the personnel function (.10*). Few of the results for both labour turnover and grievances are significant with the smaller samples, so we will not discuss them again. For the present, we should note that HR practices do not appear to have any direct effect on employee relations outcomes. The results for size may indicate that larger organisations have more formal systems in place. The negative link to a personnel professional (defined here as a personnel specialist rather than a member of the CIPD) is more difficult to explain, but could simply indicate that they are more likely to collect and retain accurate measures of these outcomes.

This initial set of findings is a strong endorsement of the model linking HRM and performance. It should be noted that HR practices have no direct link to performance. Instead, it is an indirect link through their apparent impact on employee commitment, quality and flexibility. These in turn are linked to performance outcomes. This initial set of results confirms the importance of using a greater number of progressive HR practices. The next step is to go beyond typical studies by incorporating a measure of the effective use of these practices.

Effectiveness of HRM and performance

This second analysis is a repeat of the first, with the addition of the two further measures described in Chapter 3 and designed to capture the effectiveness of both HR practices and the HR department. The results for the extended model, incorporating ratings of effectiveness, are shown in Figure 12.

Figure 12 | HRM and performance, taking into account ratings of HR effectiveness (610 HR managers)

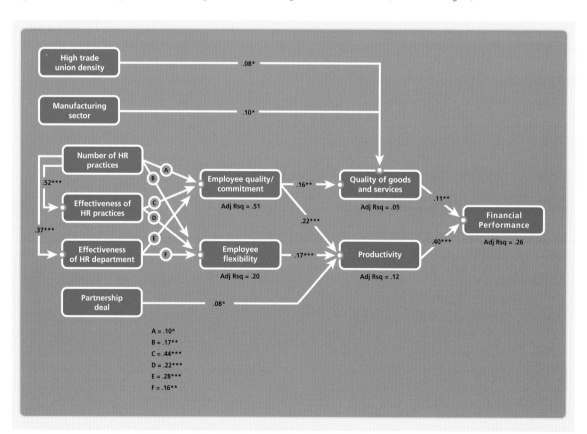

Note: * significant (p<0.05); ** strongly significant (p<0.01); *** very strongly significant (p<0.001).

"**Effectiveness of HR processes in particular and also the HR department have a significant effect on employee commitment, contribution and flexibility.**"

The results summarised in Figure 12 confirm the pattern of results shown in the previous analysis. However, they also show that effectiveness of HR processes in particular and also the HR department have a significant effect on employee commitment, contribution and flexibility. The only other change is that trade union membership falls out of the equation. It is worth noting that while HR practices are still significantly associated with commitment, quality and flexibility, the size of the association is considerably lower than in Figure 11.

Our model in Chapter 2 suggested that effectiveness would 'mediate' the relationship between HR practices and performance. This implies that HR practices would have a stronger association with outcomes if they were rated effective. We conducted a further test to explore this and the results confirm a mediation effect. In other words, by adding in the measures of HR effectiveness, we have improved our ability to explain the relationship between HRM and performance. This confirms the value of incorporating the measures of effectiveness and indicates that it is not only what you do but the way that you do it that matters.

HRM and performance (the matched sample of 237 HR managers and CEOs)

The third analysis is based on the subset of 237 HR managers whose responses can be matched to the CEO responses in the same organisation. This is a somewhat different analysis because it can incorporate the information about the firms' business strategy that was provided in the CEO questionnaire. We therefore include information on business and HR strategy and HR integration, and start by undertaking an analysis exploring the

background factors that appear to determine the take-up of HR practices and levels of HR effectiveness.

This stage of the analysis is not very revealing. Background factors such as size, sector, ownership, trade union presence and business strategy explain only a very small proportion of the uptake of HR practices or the assessment of the effectiveness of these practices. To be more specific, none of the background factors made any difference in explaining how many practices would be adopted. An HR strategy was more likely to be found where there was a personnel specialist rather than another kind of manager responsible for HR, and also, surprisingly, in smaller organisations. Human resources were more likely to be integrated into the organisation where there was a high trade union presence and in smaller organisations but to be less well integrated where the business strategy emphasised cost control.

In our model, the effectiveness of HR practices and HR departments is viewed as a consequence of HR strategy and practices as well as other background factors. When we take these into account, and in line with the mediation effect, the more HR practices in place and the higher the level of integration of HR, then the more positive the ratings of the effectiveness of HR practices and the HR department. The presence of an HR professional in charge of the department is also associated with a more effective department.

In summary, information on business and HR strategy and strategic integration is only partly helpful. It suggests that in this study at least, background factors are rather unimportant in helping to explain why HR practices are more or less likely to be adopted but we have some insight into the basis on which HR practices and departments are considered more or less effective.

The next stage was to conduct the full analysis of HRM and performance with the 237 HR managers to determine whether business and HR strategy had an effect on the results. Perhaps we should start by noting that if we repeat the main analysis reported above and presented in Figures 11 and 12 with the smaller sample, the results are almost identical. The only change is that since the sample is somewhat smaller, some of the relationships that

were significant before now cease to be significant. The results incorporating a measure of business strategy are shown in Figure 13.

This analysis shows no direct link between HR practices and outcomes. However, there is a link to effectiveness where the greater use of practices is associated with greater effectiveness. So HR practices have an indirect effect on HR outcomes. The model is generally less successful in explaining links between HRM and performance. For example, employee commitment and contribution show no link to internal performance outcomes

Figure 13 | HRM and performance – matched samples of HR managers

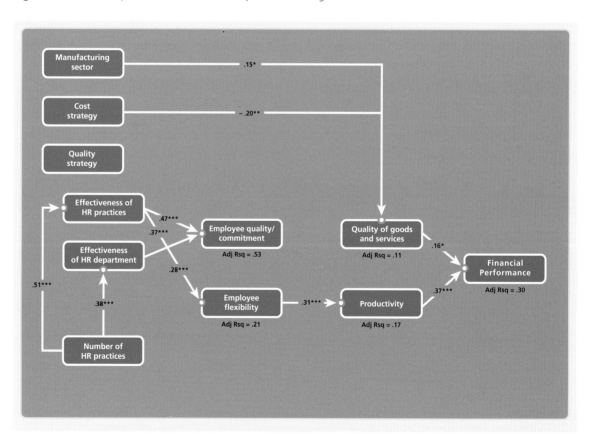

Note: * significant (p<0.05); ** strongly significant (p<0.01); *** very strongly significant (p<0.001).

such as productivity, although employee flexibility does. It is also worth noting that organisations that emphasise a cost-based strategy report a lower quality of goods and services.

HRM and performance: the assessment by the CEOs

In this key section of the analysis, the accounts of HR practices are provided by the HR managers, while all of the assessments of strategy, effectiveness and outcomes are provided by the CEOs. This is an important test since it assumes

that HR managers are in the best position to judge whether HR practices are present, while CEOs are the best judges of effectiveness and of organisational performance. Our initial analysis indicated that HR practices on their own have no impact on any outcomes as judged by CEOs. We therefore incorporate the measures of effectiveness in the full analysis shown below. The results are summarised in Figure 14.

The analysis shows no association of any sort between the adoption of HR practices, based on information collected from those responsible for

Figure 14 | HRM and performance – CEO responses

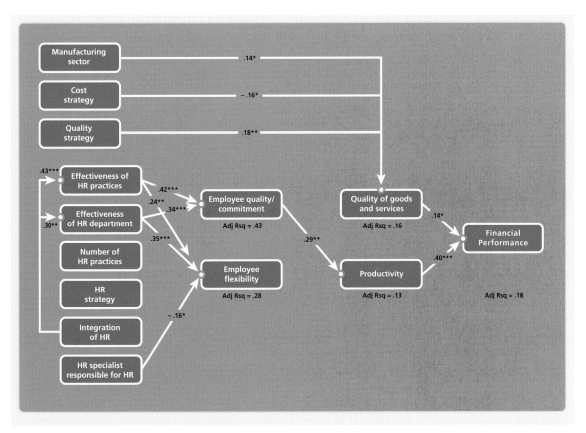

Note: * significant (p<0.05); ** strongly significant (p<0.01); *** very strongly significant (p<0.001).

> "These results confirm the importance of *effective* HR practices, an issue that has been neglected in much of the research on HRM and performance."

HR, and the outcomes reported by the CEOs. There is also no link between HR strategy or the degree of HR integration and any outcomes, although the level of integration of HR is associated with higher ratings of effectiveness of HR. These results differ from the results reported on previous pages and from those in a number of other studies, so they raise a number of questions to which we will return. However, the analysis does reveal a number of other positive links. They can be summarised as follows:

◘ Employee commitment and contribution is higher where CEOs believe there are more effective HR practices and a more effective personnel department.

◘ Employee flexibility is higher where CEOs believe there are effective HR practices and an effective personnel department but, surprisingly, not where there is an HR specialist responsible for HRM (as determined by who responded to our interview as the senior person responsible for HR).

◘ Productivity levels compared with key competitors are higher in those organisations where there are high levels of employee commitment and contribution. Nothing else we measured explains variations in CEO ratings of productivity.

◘ Quality of goods and services compared with key competitors is higher where there is a quality strategy for the organisation, it is lower where the business strategy focuses more on costs and it is higher, more generally, in the manufacturing rather than the services sector.

◘ Financial performance compared with key competitors is higher where there is higher comparative productivity and quality.

These results confirm the importance of *effective* HR practices, an issue that, as noted above, has been neglected in much of the research on HRM and performance. An effective personnel department is also important, although it should be noted that the two effectiveness measures are highly correlated. However, the absence of any effect for the number of practices adopted and the failure to find any clear 'bundles' leaves us in the dark about which practices to emphasise. Instead, the implication is that in the view of the CEOs, HR quality is more important than quantity. Another important point to emphasise is that CEOs link employee commitment and contribution at least as strongly as, if not more than, business strategy to performance outcomes. There is also an interesting contrast with HR managers who report a link between flexibility and productivity, while CEOs report a link between employee commitment and contribution and productivity. Both groups indicate a negative link between a cost-based strategy and quality of goods and services. For CEOs, there is also a positive link between a quality-focused strategy and the quality of goods and services. While this provides some general support for the model, it also indicates a stronger link between strategic focus and outcomes than some other studies have reported. One implication is that we need to continue to include a measure of strategic focus in our studies of HRM and performance. A more practical point is that the results do not offer much support for the idea of strategic choice. Rather, they indicate benefits for a quality-focused strategy and negative outcomes associated with a cost-based strategy.

Why do HR managers and CEOs provide different results?

One of the intriguing outcomes of this analysis is that the results depend partly on who you ask. While we would expect some variation in responses, the differences with respect to the presence of an HR strategy and the use of benchmarking, and the different links between use of more HR practices and outcomes are larger than we might have expected. To seek an explanation, one initial step is to explore the correlations between the responses of HR managers and CEOs. These are generally low. They are statistically significant (at the 1 per cent level) for the presence of an HR strategy (r = .267), for HR integration (r = .189) and for employee commitment and contribution (r = .262), but lower and not significant at this level for effectiveness of HR practices (r = .100) and effectiveness of the HR department (r = .099) and lowest of all for flexibility (r = .072).

These correlations suggest low levels of agreement on the potentially sensitive issue of the effectiveness of HR practices and of the HR department. More surprisingly, they are lowest of all for the measure of employee flexibility, suggesting that managers may use the term to mean rather different things. This failure to agree on assessments of key aspects of management behaviour and organisational performance implies low levels of general management integration and a low level of consensus about performance indicators. This is despite some use of benchmarking and it means that we have to treat all results with some caution.

We could speculate on reasons for the differences. One possible explanation is that those responsible for HR have more 'hands-on' or tacit knowledge about the implementation, value and success of HR practices than the CEOs. For example, they may have more information about communication difficulties, worker resistance and reactions to practices. The HR managers might have more insight into what 'works', so to speak. In contrast, the CEOs would tend to see the outcomes of HR practices rather more than the processes behind them.

In one important sense the results from HR managers and CEOs are consistent. They both show a link from effective HR practices to aspects of employee attitudes and behaviour, such as commitment and flexibility, and from this to organisational outcomes, such as higher comparative productivity and, in turn, higher financial performance. One implication is that we are identifying a form of internal consistency. Both sets of managers believe that a relationship between a committed, high quality, high performance workforce and various organisational outcomes exists; but they report this on their own terms. Furthermore, pairs of managers from the same organisation, while they may believe that such a pattern exists, do not consistently share a view of whether such a relationship is actually present in their own organisation. Put another way, in the same organisation, one manager may say there is low HR effectiveness, low employee commitment and contribution, low productivity and low financial performance while another senior manager from the same organisation is taking the opposite view. Both see a link but their judgement about whether the link is working positively or negatively differs. Of course in most cases the differences are not so extreme, nor is there any consistent trend for the CEO or HR manager to be more positive or negative. But the responses are sufficiently different to raise questions about the level of shared understanding among managers. This leads to the intriguing question of whose judgement is right. This may become easier to assess when we have the independent financial information that will be included in the next report.

Summary

While the lack of agreement between the pairs of managers and the failure of CEOs to support a direct link from HR practices to outcomes leads us to be cautious about the results, an important positive outcome is that both CEOs and HR managers indicate an association between effective HR practices, a committed, flexible workforce and high productivity and sound financial performance. On this basis, the results can be interpreted as support for the view that HR practices and their effectiveness and employee behaviour help to account for variations in the levels of company productivity and financial performance.

5 | Discussion and Conclusions

☒ **These findings reinforce the findings of the Workplace Employee Relations Survey (WERS) 1998 in showing that HR practices are not well established in the majority of workplaces.**

☒ **This report emphasises the need for an effectiveness measure in the analysis of the HRM–performance link.**

☒ **Results confirm the widespread perception that a committed and motivated workforce is crucial for business performance.**

☒ **Both HR managers and CEOs agree that more effective HR practices are associated with company economic performance.**

This report presents the initial findings from the first part of a larger study. Furthermore, it only presents selected findings within the context of the model exploring the link between human resource management (HRM) and performance. It is therefore only the first part of a larger story. The information on HRM and on other aspects of management policy and practice forms a core part of the larger study. The information on performance presented in this report is provided by the managers themselves. While this is important and useful – their subsequent policies will often be based on these judgements – it is open to criticism because it can differ from more systematic and reliable measures of firms' financial and other kinds of performance. A further stage of the study will be to incorporate this information. With this proviso, what can we learn from the survey results?

This is possibly the largest study conducted to date in the UK of company-level human resource (HR) policy and practice. It reinforces the findings of the establishment-level Workplace Employee Relations Survey in showing that HR practices are not well embedded in a majority of workplaces. While most firms report that they apply some practices – and it would be very hard for them not to be doing so – few have put in place a coherent range of practices of the sort commonly associated with 'high commitment' or 'high performance' HRM.

The absence of these practices is puzzling for two reasons. The first is the indication from the findings of a consistent belief, stronger among the HR managers than the CEOs, but present in important ways with both, that the use of more HR practices is associated with a committed, flexible and high-performing workforce that in turn is associated with higher ratings of internal performance, such as productivity and quality, and external indicators, such as financial results.

The second reason why the results are puzzling is the strong link between the use of more HR practices and ratings of the effectiveness of both HR practices in general and the HR department as a unit. Since effectiveness is strongly associated with the various outcomes, it would be logical to pursue effectiveness by introducing more practices or applying existing practices more widely. In relation to this, it is also worth emphasising that ratings of effectiveness were generally low.

> "**In most other studies, attention has been focused on whether practices are in place rather than whether they are effective.**"

The evidence about the important role played by ratings of effectiveness is one of the key findings of this study. In most other studies, attention has been focused on whether practices are in place rather than whether they are effective. This report emphasises the need to incorporate an effectiveness measure into the analysis of the HRM-performance link.

A further important outcome of this analysis is general support for the model of the relationship between HRM and performance presented at the start of this report. One of its aims is to 'open the black box' that has been created by studies exploring HRM and performance without seeking to explain how they might be linked. The model used here proposes a link through the effectiveness of practices, their impact on employee attitudes and behaviour and through these to internal and then external performance indicators. Because this is a cross-sectional study, it can only show an association and not confirm that the HR practices caused the employee responses and firm performance. However, more particularly with the full sample of 610 HR managers, that association is there. The model has utility. While the results for the smaller matched sample of CEOs are a little less convincing, key elements of the model still operate. The results therefore reinforce a widespread perception among managers that a committed and motivated workforce is crucial to high company performance.

Such results support a key role for HRM and for a focus on employees for successful economic performance. Of course in themselves they tell us little about employee reactions. Levels of employee commitment and motivation were assessed by managers. Although there is invariably a high correlation between commitment and job satisfaction, it is possible that workers might tell a rather different story. In this context, it is disappointing that the information on outcomes such as labour turnover, absence and grievances was relatively uninformative. The various background measures, including HR practices and their effectiveness, appear to have little influence on variations in these employee relations outcomes. One reason for this might be that despite the relatively positive ratings for effectiveness of personnel information, knowledge about levels of labour turnover and more particularly absence was very poor – or at least was not to hand when the interviews were conducted.

While many of the results of this study are encouraging, we failed to find any 'bundles' of HR practices and therefore resorted to use of a count of the number of practices in place. It is therefore unclear which practices are having an effect and whether there is a distinctive set of 'best' practices. There is scope to refine this measure to tap 'soft' or 'hard' measures of HRM. Of greater concern was the difference in response between the CEOs and HR managers. On a number of what might be expected to be straightforward issues, there was only a low level of agreement. These include whether or not there is an HR strategy, although sceptics might argue that the concept of strategy is always problematic. The same is true of the existence of benchmarking. Most importantly, while HR managers reported a clear link between the greater use of HR practices and outcomes, CEOs did not report better performance where HR managers indicated that more practices were in place. This may be because CEOs do not see a link between HRM and performance or – and on the basis of the data this seems more likely – CEOs and HR managers do not agree on what practices are in place. It should be emphasised that similar findings indicating low levels of agreement have

"**A further important outcome of this analysis is general support for the model of the relationship between HRM and performance presented at the start of this report.**"

been reported in a number of other studies, both in the USA and the UK. Nevertheless, they are a cause for concern both for what they say about a shared understanding among senior managers in the same organisation and because they lead us to be even more cautious about research findings based on this type of survey where there is no independent confirmation of what is really happening in the organisations. The case studies will be able to shed some light on this issue.

In summary, therefore, these preliminary results, to which we have attached a number of necessary provisos, tend to support the model linking HRM and performance. They reveal wide variations in the extent to which HR practices are applied and rather low levels of HR effectiveness. Both HR managers and CEOs agree that more effective HR practices are associated with superior company economic performance. For those that do have in place a comprehensive set of HR practices, this suggests that they may well gain considerable competitive advantage. For those who do not, the results provide an argument for treating HRM more seriously. As the next stages of the study unfold, we will be able to confirm whether or not this is indeed the case.

References

BARTLETT C. and GOSHALL S. (1989)

Managing Across Borders. Boston, Hutchinson.

BECKER B. and GERHART B. (1996)

'The impact of human resource management on organisational performance: progress and prospects'. Academy of Management Journal. Vol. 39, No. 4. pp779–801.

BECKER B., HUSELID M., PICKUS P. and SPRATT M. (1997)

'HR as a source of shareholder value: research and recommendations'. Human Resource Management. Vol. 36, No. 1. pp39–47.

COLLINS J. and PORRAS J. (1994)

Built to Last: Successful habits of visionary companies. New York, Harper Business.

CULLY M., WOODLAND S., O'REILLY A. and DIX G. (1999)

Britain at Work. London, Routledge.

DELERY J. and DOTY D. H. (1996)

'Modes of theorizing in strategic human resource management: tests of universalistic, contingency and configurational performance predictions'. Academy of Management Journal. Vol. 39, No. 4. pp802–35.

GUEST D. E. (1987)

'Human resource management and industrial relations'. Journal of Human Management Studies. Vol. 24, No. 5. pp503–21.

GUEST D. E. (1997)

'Human resource management and performance: a review and research agenda'. International Journal of Human Resource Management. Vol. 8, No. 3. pp265–76.

GUEST D. E. and HOQUE K. (1994)

'The good, the bad and the ugly: human resource management in new non-union establishments'. Human Resource Management Journal. Vol. 5, No. 1. pp1–14.

GUEST D. E. and HOQUE K. (1996)

'Human resource management and the new industrial relations'. In I. Beardwell (ed.), Contemporary Industrial Relations, Oxford, Oxford University Press.

GUEST D. E., MICHIE J., SHEEHAN M. and CONWAY N. (2000)

Employment Relations, HRM and Business Performance: An analysis of the 1998 Workplace Employee Relations Survey. Issues in People Management. London, Institute of Personnel and Development.

HUSELID M. (1995)

'The impact of human resource management practices on turnover, productivity and corporate financial performance'. Academy of Management Journal. Vol. 38. pp635–70.

ICHNIOWSKI C., SHAW K. and PRENNUSHI G. (1994)

'The effects of human resource management practices on productivity'. Working paper. New York, Columbia University.

MACDUFFIE J. P. (1995)

'Human resource bundles and manufacturing performance: flexible production systems in the world auto industry'. Industrial Relations and Labor Review. Vol. 48. pp197–221.

PATTERSON M., WEST M., LAWTHOM R. and NICKELL S. (1997)

The Impact of People Management Practices on Business Performance. Issues in People Management. London, Institute of Personnel and Development.

PFEFFER J. (1994)

Competitive Advantage through People. Boston, HBS Press.

PFEFFER J. (1998)

The Human Equation. Boston, HBS Press.

RICHARDSON R. and THOMPSON M. (1999)

The Impact of People Management Practices on Business Performance: A literature review. Issues in People Management. London, Institute of Personnel and Development.

WALTON R. (1985)

'From control to commitment in the workplace'. Harvard Business Review. Vol. 63, No. 2. pp77–84.

Appendix

The full set of human resource practices (all responses in %)

RECRUITMENT AND SELECTION	Never	Rarely	Sometimes	Often	Always	Don't know
How often does your recruitment process generate as many good/qualified applicants as you need?	0	7	31	46	13	2

	Yes	No	Don't know			
Is there a deliberate attempt to provide a preview of what work in the organisation will be like, including the more negative aspects, as part of the recruitment and selection process?	69	30	1			

	None	1–50%	51–99%	All		
What percentage of all permanent recruits are given a performance, ability or personality test as part of the selection process?	53	23	6	17		

TRAINING AND DEVELOPMENT	None	1–50%	51–99%	All		
Approximately what percentage of employees in the positions that your organisation recruits for in the largest numbers has received some form of planned training, either on or off the job, during the past year?	3	22	24	51		

	0	1–5	6–10	11–20	20+	
How many days of training does a new employee for the same position typically receive in the first year of employment?	2	35	15	12	35	
How many days a year does an experienced employee in that position typically receive?	13	50	13	6	17	

If experienced employees receive some training:	None	1–50%	51–99%	All		
Approximately what percentage is concerned with their present job?	13	25	30	31		
Approximately what percentage is concerned with their future development?	37	49	8	7		

APPRAISAL						
Approximately what percentage of your non-managerial employees:	None	1–50%	51–99%	All		
regularly (eg quarterly or annually) has their performance formally appraised?	23	16	7	54		
regularly has a proportion of their pay determined by a performance appraisal?	61	14	5	20		
regularly receives feedback on job performance from multiple sources – for example from superiors, customers, etc?	29	20	10	41		

FINANCIAL FLEXIBILITY

Percentage of non-managerial employees covered by:

	None	1–50%	51–99%	All
A system of individual performance-related pay	66	15	6	13
A system of group or team-based rewards	66	14	6	14

If yes to either or both:

	None	1–50%	51–99%	All
Percentage added to basic pay for employees covered by either an individual or a group scheme	11	85	2	1
Percentage of employees eligible for some form of cash incentive plans	67	16	5	11
Percentage of employees eligible for some form of profit-related payments or bonuses	52	9	6	33
Percentage of employees eligible for some form of deferred profit-related payments or bonuses	85	5	1	9
Percentage of employees eligible for some form of SAYE share-option scheme	85	3	2	10
Percentage of employees eligible for some form of executive share-option scheme	95	4	0	1

JOB DESIGN

	None	1–50%	51–99%	All
Percentage of employees working in self-managed teams	49	32	10	9
Percentage of employees working in cross-function teams	47	39	7	7
Percentage of employees working in project-based teams	47	47	4	3
Percentage of employees having flexible job descriptions	28	28	12	32
Percentage of employees whose jobs are deliberately designed to make full use of their skills and abilities	38	30	14	19
Percentage of employees qualified or capable to perform more than one job	4	49	33	15
Percentage of employees who have access to flexible work arrangements	64	28	2	6

TWO-WAY COMMUNICATION

	None	1–50%	51–99%	All
Percentage of employees who receive formal information on business operations and performance	24	18	4	54
Percentage of employees distributed formal surveys that ask for their views and opinions	62	11	1	26

	No	Yes
Information on business plans is regularly provided to all employees	57	43
Information on the firm's performance targets is provided to all employees	40	60
Information on performance results is provided to all employees	33	67
Mechanisms to inform employees about important new initiatives	18	82
Mechanisms to consult employees on organisation's business plan	57	43
Employees or their representatives are consulted before performance targets are set	63	37

EMPLOYMENT SECURITY/INTERNAL LABOUR MARKET

	None	1–50%	51–99%	All
Percentage of non-entry level vacancies filled from within over the last three years	14	61	20	4

	No	Yes
The organisation promotes from within whenever possible	11	89
The organisation is committed to employment security	25	75
Have voluntary redundancies occurred in the past three years?	66	34
Have compulsory redundancies occurred in the past three years?	45	55

SINGLE STATUS AND HARMONISATION

	No	Yes
Harmonised holiday entitlement for all employees	17	83
Harmonised maternity and sick leave entitlements for all employees	13	87
A common pension scheme for all employees	36	64
The same canteen and/or eating arrangements for all employees	22	78
A formal commitment for achieving single status	53	47

QUALITY

	None	1–50%	51–99%	All
Percentage of employees participating regularly in employee problem-solving groups	32	49	10	9
Percentage of employees participating regularly in quality circles	48	40	6	5
Percentage of employees participating regularly in work improvement teams	46	42	6	6

	None	Not much	A fair amount	A lot	Full
Level of responsibility of employees in ensuring the quality of their own work	0	1	19	45	35